I0201647

Working With the Negatives

Poems by Steven Storrie

Copyright © 2016 by Steven Storrie

Layout: Pski's Porch
Cover design: Pski's Porch

All rights reserved. No part of this book may be re-
produced in any form by any electronic or mechanical
means including photocopying, recording, or informa-
tion storage and retrieval without permission in writing
from the author.

ISBN-13: 978-0-9978706-2-6
ISBN-10: 0997870621

for more books, visit Pski's Porch:
www.pskisporch.com

Printed in U.S.A

for Danielle, who always believed

Contents

part 1

part 1

part 1

"One day you might get so far out you won't come back at all"
— William Burroughs

"Hit me, baby, one more time"
— Britney Spears

WHAT HAPPENS WHEN STRIPPERS BLOW THEIR KNEES OUT PART ONE

I slump home to my crumby apartment
On a downtown Chicago train
Not together
Apart
Ready to channel surf
And eat my KFC.

A guy on the street
Wears a 'True Blue'
Madonna t-shirt and a sign that says
'Change'

I toss him the spare change I have
And tell him I agree.

JOHN WAYNE MOVIES

My Grandfather only ever liked two things
Fishing and John Wayne movies
He would always say that fishing relaxed him
But there was never the promise
That you would catch anything
Life is so full of uncertainties
He'd tell me as a child
More and more there are no guarantees
At least in John Wayne movies
He'd say
You know who's gonna fucking win.

VLADIMIR PUTIN LOOKS GOOD IN THOSE HEELS

Shoulders like Mt Rushmore
A head like the Great Plains
A back like Oklahoma and
Chest like the Hoover Dam

Fists like the Colorado Rapids
Eyes like the economy
Guts like the Constitution

Arms like California
And legs like New York.

100 proof vodka
And nobody in the world to rein him in

Man, Vladimir Putin
Sure looks good in those
Heels.

REAGAN ERA TATTOOS

I got these tattoos when
Ronald Reagan was President
When Wall Street was flooded with
Money
And it was every man for
Himself

When Madonna, Prince and Michael Jackson
Filled our music televisions
And E.T told us what really happened
To Christ

I got them while Ron was in the White House
And Ferris Bueller was bunking off
I had them while the Breakfast Club sat detention
And we bombed the shit of Haiti
Just to show them who's boss

I got one for Ally Sheedy
And one for that chick in Splash!
I got one for John Lennon
Whose death ushered in the decade

Looking back on it with hindsight
I suppose we should have fucking known.

There's a tattoo dedicated to John Rambo
And to Ted Turner's CNN
Who is gonna watch a news channel

We all said
24 hours a day?

You got one that said airhead
And I got one that said 'Bad To The Bone'
They were radical phrases back then, babe
Radical

I got one of my favourite Ninja Turtle
Eating a slice of pizza
And never even questioned what a weird premise that is
How could I?
I was too busy learning to skateboard
And fumbling with that Rubik Cube
Wondering what AIDS was and how to avoid it
And hating those Commie Russian bastard sons of bitches

One or two of them were healing
Through Grenada
And Tiananmen Square
And while the Berlin Wall fell down.

At least these faded tattoos lasted longer
Than New Coke and the Challenger shuttle
I suppose

I got a couple while watching the Iran-Contra affair unfold
While goofy old Ronnie built his Star Wars thing
Never letting on for one second
That America's favourite Grandpa
Was a lying sack of shit

If I could change one thing about the 80's
It wouldn't be these tattoos

It wouldn't be shoulder pads or the shitty drugs
No
It would be that Hinckley
Never fucking missed.

HOLLYWOOD TYPES

They'll sell you, Lloyd.
At least, that's what I thought she said.
She looked at me with a face like curdled milk.
She wore expensive clothes, expensive jewellery
Had an expensive handbag
And reeked of expensive perfume
I had a yoghurt stain on my shirt
Crumbs in my beard
And had strayed onto her patch
What do you mean, I asked
The film she replied testily
She was getting impatient
And I was wasting her time
Of your book
How would you like to be
On celluloid?

Oh, I scoffed derisively

These Hollywood types

I liked my version better.

BUSH ERA TATTOOS

I got these tattoos when
George W. Bush was President
When there was a war on something called
Terror
The Patriot Act, WMD's and Guantanamo
And nobody knew
what the fuck was going on

The leader of the free world
Didn't care about black people
A singer said
And was secretly glad to see them getting washed away
His brother liked to hang with a guy named Chad
In Florida
Or something
And together they pulled off the greatest robbery
The country had ever seen

Hadn't he been an alcoholic in his youth?
A waste of skin and space?
Someone best thrown onto a Nascar track
At the Indy 500
And left to fend for himself?
A man who, when faced with the prospect of war
In some place they called 'Nam
had ran to his over indulgent Daddy
Who told him with the conviction of
One who had done so many times before
Don't worry, son

Money will get you out of this.

In my mind I see him in a classroom
Reading to kids all seated beneath him
Kids who probably read at a higher level
Than he did
All wondering who the fuck this old guy was
Who couldn't get his mouth around
6th grade words.
Who held the book like it was a foreign object
And kept stammering like he was caught in a lie
I see the aide lean in and tell him the news
The news that changed everything
Changed the world
The news coming out of New York City
Something about two planes and the World Trade Centre
He sits
And he sits
And he sits
A glazed look on his face
Wondering if Spot the dog
Is ever gonna catch that ball
Before someone in the Secret Service
Says to him in a whisper
Mr President
Don't you think we'd better go?

I can still see him standing at Ground Zero
Stood atop the rubble
Of concrete and steel
Revelling in feeling like
One of the boys
One of the regular Joe's
Who'd buy him a beer

If he ever wandered into their bar
On the corner of some cold street
In the middle of downtown Pittsburgh
He's crowing into a megaphone
Arm draped around someone
Hired from the lines
Of a Bruce Springsteen song
In order to denote authenticity
And show he's one of us
His bemused look has faded
Now he's enjoying himself
He thinks it's a deleted scene
From a new Bruce Willis movie
As his head cranks up
He's playing to the crowd
He hears us, he says
The rest of the world
Can hear us too
And the people who knocked these buildings down
Will hear all of us
Soon.

Somewhere in a room that wreaks of leather furniture
And the vilest abuses of power
Dick Cheney is laughing his ass off
Slugging 100 year old whiskey
And abusing the Thai houseboy

I got these tattoos
When George W. Bush was President.

ON WATCHING THE UCLA WOMENS GYMNAST TEAM

I spend Saturday night alone
With a bucket of greasy chicken
And cold beer to wash down the chips
To expedite some kind of sorry ending
Or distort my appearance
Just a little more
Sitting in my shorts
Waiting for my phone to light up
Fingers staining my book
I watch the UCLA gymnasts move
In that incredible way women can move
And wonder just when it was
Everything
got quite
So fucked up.

KANYE WEST IS DEAD

There's war somewhere on foreign soil
The kids next door are smoking foil
My father sinks in heavy toil
And Kanye West is dead

The factory closed, we're on the shelf
All we want is a little help
There's guys out there can't feed themselves
And Kanye West is dead.

The bankers' robbed us, stole our homes
I say it once this system's broke
Donald Trump I hope you choke
Kanye West is dead

The school I went to just went under
Protesters scream for blood and thunder
It's enough to make you wonder
And Kanye West is dead

On my street a boy was knocked from his bike
He turned left and the car turned right
It got 100 Facebook likes
But Kanye West is dead

The candidates play racist Pacman
You vote for them you know what happens
The wheels are coming off this wagon
Kanye West is dead

Kim Kardashain and Kendall Jenner
Wipe their ass on crisp new tenners
I can't see it getting better
Now Kanye West is dead

Whose are those eyebrows on the cover of Vogue?
What? Are you crazy? Don't you know?!
I guess I must be getting old
And Kanye West is dead

Tell me where you bought those ears
I drink vodka because it's clear
I don't recall how I got here
But Kanye West is dead

I want to smash this dumb culture
Nothing here but pouting vultures
Who gives a fuck who doesn't love ya?
Kanye West Is dead.

Remember when we loved this town?
When all our dreams were golden brown
What was it, then, that tore us down?
Kanye West is dead

My ex-girlfriend's losing hope
A single mother that just can't cope
She's at the end of a fraying rope
And Kanye West is dead.

When we were young and we were free
We knew who we'd grow to be
But it's too dark for us to see
Now Kanye West is dead.

The girl next door is brash and bold
Pregnant again with her fourth
She's just turned 15 years old
And she knows
Kanye West is dead

It's on the front of all the papers
Instagram and Twitter pages
Not the teen whose father raped her
But that Kanye West is dead

It's hard to tell what really matters
When your illusions lay in tatters
When you're not famous your ego shatters
Like Kanye West, who's dead.

Here we stand in a brave new world
Stripped of dreams, cold and scared
I can't believe you haven't heard
Kanye West is dead

So nothing left but empty roads
All those you once thought would stay will go
Looks like you'll have to face this alone
Kanye West is dead

It's almost over that's a fact
We might have known this wouldn't last
But cheer loud enough, scream and clap
Can you hear me at the back?

That Kanye West
He's dead.

CHARLES BUKOWSKI'S BROKEN KNUCKLE

On the toilet bowl
In the library
There is a shit stain
From the last old man
To sit here
And a glory hole
Through which
A wrinkled cock
With a swollen
Purple
Head
Pokes through
Begging to be pleased

I leap up in disgust
And leave in a stream of foul obscenities
A letter awaits me when I get home
From a former employer
Claiming I owe them 11 grand
In overpaid salaries
Them getting that money
Or me using the library facilities again
It's impossible to say
Which will happen first.

WHEN REDNECKS SHOOT OUT THE WINDOWS
OF YOUR AUTOMOBILE YOU KNOW
YOU'RE DOING SOMETHING RIGHT

On the street two old women
Slowly pass me by talking about
Donald Trump
I'm going to vote for him
One says
I want him to build that wall
Keep these Mexicans out
The other one
The oldest if you can believe it
Nods in thoughtful agreement
I'm voting for him too
She says
I want to see this ban on Muslims
Entering America

The sun hits my face in disbelief
I'm standing on the Grassy Knoll
In Dallas, Texas
Wondering where Lee Harvey Oswald is
Now we really need him.

ADVICE FOR MY UNBORN SON

I move on the sofa
Whisper into his mother's swollen belly
I tell him to get through as many books
As possible
And always to box
Because a man who is well read and can hit hard
Is a dangerous man indeed

JENNY, YOU'RE EXCUSED

You entered my life like
A rock through glass
Wearing nothing but tiny
Summer dresses and
A clean pair of heels

You left my life like
Wet leaves down a clogged drain
Washed away in the storm floods
Looking far less prettier
Than when you first came
Crisp
Breathless
Aglow
The promise of something better
Dripping from your tongue

The bit in the middle is called life
Don't feel bad
It gets everybody
In the end.

LAST EXIT TO NOWHERE

I remember how years ago
My wife bought me a copy of
Hubert Selby Jr's book
Last Exit To Brooklyn
To help you
She said
With your writing
At that time I was very sensitive
about telling people I was writing
That I was a writer
Even though I suppose I was
By definition

I began reading it almost immediately
on the train home
She was my girlfriend back then
Lived four hours from me
Was at college in a strange new town
I was recently returned from Atlanta
Having given up most everything to be with her
And was rewarded with her protecting and encouraging
the pursuit of my fragile dream
If I hadn't known it before
(and I had, of course)
She was the one for me.

My life was fairly easy at this time
Untouched by the troubles that would come later
And I wrote with appropriate gusto

Most of it was lightweight shit, of course
I wasn't yet ready
You must go through the white heat of the furnace
To become porcelain
And
soon enough
I would

I remember it was the introduction
That made the biggest impression on me
First time around
Selby Jr talked about how tough his life was at that point
Married with kids and a full time job
He broke down the details of his writing habits
Coming home from work and starting the real task of his day
Of writing
Of roaming
Of trying to capture that thing

I was transfixed by two little sentences
That detailed how tight the walls were closing in on him
Looking after 4 people on $70 a week
About how he would take off his suit and tie
Try acting like a husband for a while
Before retiring to his typewriter for the night

Years later things would get tight for me, too
Almost too tight
And I would think back to those lazy train rides home
When I read *Last Exit To Brooklyn*
Without really knowing what was going on
Or what it took to make it
I would trudge home in snow at 11pm
Microwave my dinner

And eat it as quietly as I could
My wife already sleeping in bed upstairs
The bills were due and I had no money
She had long since finished college in the strange new town
And now here we were in this one
Just sort of floating around
I hadn't delivered on the promise I'd made her
That we would be rich and famous and live exciting lives
Instead we slaved away in drudgery
Did the best we could
Tried to make ends meet
Like everybody else
I was sick to my heart and soul with circumstances
But had neither the gumption nor the ideas to change

So on it went

How many hours did I spend at freezing train stations?
Without a book to read
In supermarkets in the dead of night
Just trying to keep warm
Staring down strangers
With the cold and hungry eyes of a starving wolf
I bore little resemblance to who I used to be
And none to what I was trying to become

I soldiered on regardless
Going in the wrong direction
I took the off ramp to a place called 'nowhere'
Another washed up loser that didn't have the courage or the
style
I was muttering into the wrong end of a megaphone
With my face pushed up against the glass to see who was inside
When what I should have been doing is bellowing my words

Into the street
Into the stratosphere
From the top of the highest rooftop
I could find

Then I think of the book my wife gave me
Of how Hubert talks about the word 'violence'
Coming from the Latin that means 'Life Force'
I got mean through all those years
Tough
Hard
Mean
Finally I got violent
Anger awoke within me and I lashed back on the world
A raging, snarling beast
I hunted and pursued my dreams with gusto
And never took no for any kind of answer
I pushed my face to the grindstone
And bared my ribs to the crowds
I wrote with a different kind of violence

I wrote with a different kind of force.

I suppose what I'm saying is
That I'm sorry to my wife for making it so hard
But we're here now
I did it

I suppose what I'm saying is I needed those years
To get hardened
Like a boxer needs to go a few rounds
Before he knows what's really within him
You can't be the champion from just sparring
You need guts and a hard head in this game, kid

And neither one comes cheap.

I suppose what I'm saying is thanks for putting up with me
All these years
Thanks for believing
And never complaining

Thanks for the encouragement
Thanks for the love
Thanks for remaining strong throughout

And thanks for giving me a book
That time
On a cold autumnal day

COME ALL YE FAITHFUL

She peeled off her pants
Underneath the Christmas tree
Wiggling under the lights
Until I could see the hairs.

Beth could drink her egg nog
With the best of them
And put it away on Christmas Eve
Like no other time before

We fucked that night
Beneath the angel and the baubles
When it was over I told her
I hate Christmas
Yeh she replied
But what are you gonna do about it
What am I gonna do about it
I said
Face scrunched up in disgust
So I dragged the tree outside
Set it on fire
While across the street
A children's choir
Filled the crisp night air
And all the little heathens
Prayed they had been good enough
this year
to get the presents
they so richly deserved.

THE NIGHT CHARLES BUKOWSKI DRANK WITH HARRY DEAN STANTON

When I tell my Grandma that I'm a writer now
That my book is coming out
That I've finally made it
She smiles sweetly
Nods knowingly
Gazes upon me with warm, admiring eyes
You always were a good little reader
She reminds me proudly
I still remember you
Sitting on that floor of a Saturday evening
Reading the local paper out loud to me
When you were only four
Only four, she repeats emphatically
Holding up four fingers
And gesturing to the carpet floor
I look at the imaginary spot she's pointing to
And point out that more than any
Precociousness on my part
That probably says more
About the quality of writing
in the local paper
at the time.

part 1

"The ice is near, the loneliness is terrible – but how serenely every-thing lies in the sunshine! How freely one can breathe! How much, one feels, lies beneath one."

- Nietzsche

1865

He comes at me like old age
Blood rattling in his jaw
In wide eyes I see his children
Mud and death caked on his hands
I thought for a second I saw
William Tecumseh Sherman
In the lights of a downtown Georgia train

A confluence of sirens tug hard
at the sky
Once
Twice
Three times
My eyes flicker into cinematic being
At the end of a snapped off dream

The sheets are still white
Air still pervades the room
I gasp
Suck it in sharply with greed
Then wipe the sweat from my brow.

It's getting easier
I think
Not as bad
As it once used to be.

ON A COLD TUESDAY MORNING

She dangles her feet over Toronto
Cars and trucks like sick bugs beneath her
Don't you wish we could always live this way
She says
Out on the edge with nowhere left to go
Come inside
I say
And we can talk about it
She looks at me coyly
Smiles
Shifts her weight and
Swivels her legs

The hole in the skyline
Is filled back in
And I'm breathing a little easier
Than I was
A moment ago.

NEBRASKA ROADS

Her eyes were weeping like wounds
Cast in another direction
Away from me
Her mouth was closed and calm
A silent gun turret
That had spent all its shells
Those hands, soft and trembling
Were balled in calloused fists
Of empty rage
And her arms
The ones that once held me
Were like paper blotched with ink

There were mountains between us now
Distance growing as long as the Nebraska roads
Storm clouds gathered above us
Like pillows employed to block out the light
Our hearts had cracked liked vases
The truth like a baseball to glass doors
There would be no-one to pick up the
Pieces
Of this latest thing I'd done.

THE GARBAGE TRUCK IS COMING

The garbage truck is coming
Down the street at 6am
Its lights illuminate the darkness
And its noise rattles and clangs
Telling people who've been sleeping
It might be
Time for work

The men leap from the side and back
Some weary
Some strong
They've been doing this for years
And it always stays the same
Sure
You might find the odd piece of jewellery
Or a strange gift from an even stranger soul
But make no mistake
This job is monotony incarnate
And doesn't get easier as you go

You get used to the smell
They say
Stop noticing it after a week
Mostly you move at a snail's pace
And get funny looks from women
In expensive clothes
It doesn't matter that you're a poet
It doesn't matter you race bikes
In California on the weekends

And know where all the celebs like to go
It doesn't matter your life
Is more exciting than theirs
And you know things they'll never know
You're a garbage man
You'll always be a garbage man
Get used to it

I watch them drag the rubbish
From the drive to the truck
And back to the street
Their faces are blank
Most of them
Tired
And bored
And old
The young ones move with gusto
They haven't learned yet
That garbage keeps on coming
No matter how fast you try and go

I hear them banter with each other
Across the street and down the road
My wife has got the kettle on
The kitchen bathed in half light
The T.V sound turned low

The orange light is getting closer
Making its way through the dawn
The driver eases forward
Rubs his eyes and starts to yawn

Eventually they reach me
My house at the end of the block

I feel a sadness fill my heart

'Hi'
I say
The early morning cold
Blowing through my bones
'I'm the new guy
Where is it I should start?'

BASEBALL IN HAVANA

They're playing baseball in Cuba
And the President is there to watch
It was raining when he landed
And nobody thought to greet him
But he doesn't seem to hold
A grudge
He's here to extend the hand of freedom
To the Cuban people
He's here, he says, to bury
The last remnant of the Cold War
In the Americas
He's here to remove the red tape
And give Cuba the internet
Freedom of speech
New business opportunities

We've been shadow boxers
Since 1959, he tells them
But no more

Calvin Coolidge
Fidel Castro
The Missile Crisis
And The Bay of Pigs.
Not to mention that unfortunate business
With The Kennedy's.
It's history now
And so is this.

Cuba
You're not sure
He's making a deal with the devil
You say
He's not asking for anything in return
You say
He's just here on holiday with his wife and kids
Nothing has changed
We're still oppressed
See one Castro
See them all

Cuba
America has unlocked your gates
Whether you like it or not
We're friends now
It's China we don't trust.

Cuba
The Americans are coming
They're playing baseball in Havana
Better visit quickly
Before they start importing
Modern cars
And the hotels look very different
Than they did a year ago.

WHERE'S THE FRONTIER, AMY?

A storm wrecked this place last night
Torn up trees and
Overturned cars
A teddy sits in the gutter
And a photo album
Wet through and ruined
Sails along
On the trickling tide
I sit alone in a diner
At a sticky table
Nursing one coffee
And a million thoughts
The waitress looks tired
As waitresses often do
I think to smile and say hello
But don't
I drop a tip onto the plate instead
Finish my drink
Stand up
leave

I'm late for my shift at the fire station
I had to admit
My first week in the job
In this town
In this life
It hasn't been so great.

WARM HOMES & COLD BEERS

I see the workers
Trudging home
From the
Mill
Wet streets and nightfall
Headlights rushing by
In the rain
There's weariness in their bones
In their eyes
And in
Their hearts
Warm homes
Cold beers
Sport on T.V
I see them in the dawn also
The day still ahead of them
Bodies aching
Under grey skies rusted like the tracks
The flame burns through the night
And lets them know
They still have a living
Here in the steel
In the concrete
In the mud
In the grip of something
That had them before
Before they even figured
Figured out
Who they really
Were.

BORN AND RAISED

The bar is dingy
And the music doesn't fit
It's all modern pop shit
And the guys in here
Predate the fucking building
They think Sinatra is still alive
Most of them

She collects my empty glass
I remember when this place
Was the old bowling alley
I say
Making conversation
I don't remember that
She shrugs
Disinterested
In my memories
In me
I wasn't born then
She trudges away
Weary
4 hours of her shift
Still left to go.

I look at the rain sodden carpark
Headlights puncturing the dull grey drizzle
Of just another day
And wonder
If you don't recognise the places you're sitting in

If none of it looks the way it was before you left
And all the people you knew are gone.
Then
Can you really
still call it home?

HAPPINESS BY THE MILE

Didn't I crown you?
Didn't I place you on a throne?
Up there, above them all
Above even me
Out of reach
of the cold
Didn't I untangle the wires?
For you
Didn't I unclog the drains
of my heart?
Muddy black picture
For you

The thing you have to
Remember
When you're dealing with me
When I'm dealing with you
Is that it hurts
When I even try to
Speak
My signal is overwhelmed
In the colour of your noise
So I sit there rejected
Scolded
Defeated

You deflect every advance
With a mastery unbound
So I dig myself deeper

burrow further in
And wait like a sniper
Dead among the
Leaves.

3AM SOMEWHERE IN THE WORLD

The lights of the empty airport
Sting my tired eyes
And I'm left wondering why it is that
A bar in here named O'Leary's
With green walls
And framed pictures
Of Boston sports teams
Old and new
Makes me feel so lonely
Makes me feel sadder
Than I've ever felt before.

NORTHERN

I'm in the river again
Dark shades and dirty jeans
Why must I come down here
Every few months or so
With heartsick intentions and
The will to drown?
Everything looks the same
As it did the last time
Cracked ribcages and
Twisted vines
The mud it seizes my ankles
I've got work to do as usual
Better get on with it then
We don't want to still be here
When the sun finally goes down.

WINTER

There you sit on the banks of the Wishkah
Dipping your toes in, covered in mud
You call out to me as always
Your heart wrapped in a shawl
And a voice like a confluence of sirens
Taking me into the woods
Inveigling me with darkness
Sucking the sky from my window
And telling me my time is up.

Throw your rocks at me
Throw them
What damage is there left to do
We know your venom debilitates
We know your aim is true

Throw your rocks then
Throw them
My soul bears greater wounds
The scars on my flesh were pink
Then white
Time heals everything they say
Almost

One day in this muddy river
You'll throw your rocks while I
Bathe in strands of daylight
And as you cackle there in vicious glee
Tossing your head askance with the

Callous joy of it all
A noble savage is going to creep
Up behind you from the bushes
Barefoot with love in his heart
His face is going to be painted
With the blood of a thousand lovers and
Without saying a word as he raises his spear
He's gonna plunge it between your shoulder blades
He's gonna stab you in the back
And I'll carry on bathing my wounds in this vile
And muddy river
For misfortune and all of its disciples
Know not how to laugh.

THESE SNOW FILLED STREETS

How many times can you
Rebuild yourself before
It starts to take its toll?
9 is my guess but
I suppose we'll have to
Wait
and see.

DOWN IN A HOLE

I had came here through a fog
Thick as bank vaults
Sweating on public transport
My feet getting wet in the rain
I was sick with despair and
the hour of the morning
The best part of me
left between the sheets

they wanted to know
my 5 year work history
with dates and addresses and names
all the shavings of my life
in a nice little plastic bag

the rain lashes the windows and
I stifle a shudder
Try not to vomit
As she hands me the pen.

What were *you* doing
5 years ago today?

GOUGE AWAY

Just one more week
And it's payday
Just one more week
And it's vacation time
Just one more week
And it's Memorial Day
A three day weekend
Thank the Lord

Soon the weeks pile up
like dead bodies
Blank faced and unaccounted for
The days like letters
Stuffed into a shoebox

What I wouldn't give
Just once
To be
King.

Steven Storrie has worked as a cable T.V repair man, dishwasher, choreographer, ice cream vendor and junk yard attendant. He can usually be found bickering with his neighbours over nothing and storing the baseballs he keeps when they are hit into his yard. This is his first collection of poetry.

Pski's Porch Publishing was formed July 2012, to make books for people who like people who like books. We hope we have some small successes.
www.pskisporch.com.

Pski's Porch

323 East Avenue
Lockport, NY 14094
www.pskisporch.com

www.ingramcontent.com/pod-product-compliance
Lightning Source LLC
Chambersburg PA
CBHW071933020426
42331CB00010B/2848